Dear
Lauren and Keith
Max and Jack:....

I pass this on to
you because your
gardens are so
special and so
spectacular
"maybe" you can
create such a book
someday!! LOVE YOU
Mimi

RUSTIC GARDEN ARCHITECTURE

RUSTIC GARDEN
ARCHITECTURE

Ralph Kylloe

GIBBS·SMITH
PUBLISHER

SALT LAKE CITY

First Edition

99 98 97 3 2 1

This is a Peregrine Smith Book,
published by Gibbs Smith, Publisher
P.O. Box 667
Layton, UT 84041

Designed by Scott Van Kampen
Edited by Gail Yngve

Printed and bound in Asia
Library of Congress Cataloging-in-Publication Data
Kylloe, Ralph R. Rustic garden architecture /
Ralph Kylloe. – 1st ed. p. cm.
ISBN 0-87905-795-5 1. Pergolas. 2. Gazebos.
3. Garden ornaments and furniture. I. Title.
NA8450.K96 1997
717–dc20 96–41831
CIP

dedication

For Leah Robinson,
daughter of rustic builder
David Robinson.
Leah has struggled for
eight of her eleven years
with a brain tumor.
May she and her family
find peace in their lives,
and may the rest of us
realize that our problems
are insignificant compared
to those who suffer with the
illness of a child.

David Robinson's gazebo serves as gateway to the Rustic Playground in Central Park.

acknowledgements

During the past several years, I have had the opportunity to write and photograph several books and dozens of articles about rustic furnishings and decor. I have also had the opportunity to lecture to many interested groups around the country on rustic style and designs, and I am a contributing editor at *Log Home Living* magazine. In addition, I am the senior design consultant at the Old Hickory Furniture Company in Shelbyville, Indiana, and I have a very large gallery in Lake George, New York, where I sell both antique and contemporary rustic furnishings and provide interior design services to a wide range of clients.

Because I have completed several books on interior rustic decor, it was only natural for me to step outside and complete a book on *Rustic Garden Architecture*. I must say that traveling to gardens all over the East Coast has been more than delightful. The gardens and settings we have seen have been extraordinary, and the individuals who opened their garden gates to us have been exceptional.

Many people should be acknowledged for their contributions to this book. Without them this book would not have been completed. I want to personally thank Marvin Davis and Robert Oleery, co-owners of Romancing the Woods in Catskill, New York. The original odd couple, these two characters are complete opposites. Their comical disagreements are the stuff of legends. Marvin handles the public relations, and Bob is responsible for production. They make wonderful garden architecture and both are consummate hosts.

I also wish to thank Lionel Maurier of Meredith, New Hampshire. Lionel has always been open with his production techniques and builds some of the best rustic furniture in the business.

David Robinson is the quintessential rustic garden furnishings builder. His pieces and structures are extraordinary. He is well known for rebuilding the marvelous gazebos in Central Park and for his high quality workmanship and attention to detail.

A deep and personal indebtedness goes to Chris Williams and Craig Campbell, co-owners of the Old Hickory Furniture Company of Shelbyville, Indiana. Their efforts have brought back the American tradition of Indiana hickory furniture, and they are great friends and business associates as well.

Also, a special thanks to Chip Kalleen, senior designer at Old Hickory. His efforts, skills and talents have made my life infinitely easier.

I want to especially thank my wife, Michele. She is the one who styles all my photographs for our books, and I could not have completed this project without her.

Finally, I wish to thank our architect Michael Bird of Saranac Lake, New York, Thad and Barbara Collum of Barbara Collum Interior Design, architect Warren Reiss of Scenic Hudson, and everybody else who took part in the completion of this book.

contents

foreword

Having explored the world of rustic furniture for the past twenty years and having written five books and more articles than I can remember on the subject, it was only natural for me to look at related artistic efforts. Rustic architecture and specifically garden structures have been around a long time. Further, just about every country in the world had some sort of folksy-rustic structures including Eskimos, Africans, Aborigines, as well as cultures that most of us are more familiar with. Rustic is a unique term that means many things to many people. *Webster's Dictionary* offers: simplicity, uncouth, unrefined, unsophisticated, and others. However, for the sake of this manuscript, rustic refers to natural materials, unaltered and not significantly modified to disguise the real nature of the material. A rustic structure, then, may be a gazebo made from logs, sticks, twigs, roots, antlers, or other natural material.

Humans have a unique capacity to create. Our own evolutionary progression may not be happening before our eyes, but our evolutionary thinking is. It is often said that there have been few significantly original thoughts in the past thousand years. Rather, ideas–like plants and trees–grow, become increasingly complex, and eventually fade away. Like life, ideas are often reborn. The essence of an idea may be structurally sound but humans are well known for their capacity to alter existing concepts and make them uniquely their own. For instance, Frank Lloyd Wright, often referred to as America's greatest and most influential architect, was profoundly influenced by Japanese architecture. Pablo Picasso, recognized as the twentieth century's most-celebrated artist and often credited with the advent of Cubism, was profoundly affected by African tribal art that, upon examination, clearly demonstrated cubist style and had been produced for hundreds of years.

Nonetheless, rustic architecture and garden structures have been around a long time. From early block prints we know that the Chinese had rustic furniture made of roots in the fourteenth century. Gardens in the mid-1700s in England, France, and Italy were filled with not only luscious plants but garden structures of all sorts. Today, the tradition of rustic garden architecture continues, and, in a sense, is enjoying revitalization. This book celebrates that revitalization.

A vine-covered arbor is often used as a place for quiet times and contemplation.

Gardens

are the respite of

humanity.
They speak of peace
and rejuvenation. They quiet the
soul and render us to solitude. They
are the earthly residences of gods,
angels, druids, gremlins, and spirits
of all kinds. Charming us with
nature's subtleties, gardens captivate
us with vibrant color. They cool us
with their mighty arms and bring
forth images of birth and rebirth.
They speak of the health and well
being of the earth and ultimately
ourselves—the garden of Eden, the
garden of earthly delight.

Home and mother to us all, the earth itself is a garden. It need not be cultivated, tampered with, or altered. It is complete in itself. Compare Earth with, say, Venus—molten rock, nine hundred degrees, no oxygen. No organic molecule could possibly survive let alone evolve. It's hell at its finest—not a friendly place to visit.

Early in human evolution we lived in gardens. The trees were our homes. We felt safe and secure from the torment of the mighty hunters of the plains. In time we built shelters in the forests, near water, where we could live our lives in peace. For thousands of generations we lived off gardens, and the beauty and resourcefulness of the forest became hard-wired into our brains.

In time we moved to the plains and built great cities. There we lived in crowded houses, worked shoulder to shoulder with our coworkers, and toiled long hours to make ends meet. It was an exhausting existence. Most of us preferred

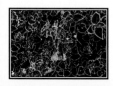 not to live that way, but we did what was necessary to survive.

A Victorian gentleman photographed standing next to a rustic gazebo located in upstate New York.

This stereo view of a rustic bridge in New York's Central Park is circa 1900.

EARLY EFFORTS

The Greeks and Romans maintained gardens. So did the Egyptians along the lush banks of the Nile. Before these cultures, the Babylonians and Sumatrans gardened. The Chinese have always loved gardens as have cultures from almost all continents, elevating their horticultural efforts to the realm of the artistic. Gardening is as old as civilization and humanity. It is an act of great care and beauty. It is a

A delightful gazebo constructed by Romancing the Woods of Woodstock, New York, resides on the banks of a lily pad-choked lake in central New York.

profound act of love and compassion.

Humans do not have to garden. Other than for the great industrial farms we would survive, probably quite well, without ornamental trees surrounding our homes, flowers in our pots, and shrubbery in our yards. But without gardens we would live in a sterile world, bereft of beauty and void of nurturing and compassion.

Gardening is an end unto itself. True, we enjoy seeing the fruits of our efforts. But the act of caring for tiny plants soothes our souls and brings peace to the turmoil in our hearts and minds.

Peace permeates the forest, a kind of peace unobtainable elsewhere.

There is harmony and grace dwelling in the gardens and the forests we so enjoy. Gardens quiet our chaos and calm our nerves.

The garden is unique because it is there that we ponder thoughts and questions. It is there we seek meaning in our lives. It is there we find answers to the great questions of our times,

and it is there we call our home.

It is not by accident that we cultivate gardens. It is not by accident that we keep pets. We are, in the most simplest and purest of all realities, part of nature ourselves. And we need to be reminded of our own unmistakable roots to the earth. Passionately, then, it is in the garden that we rediscover our past, experience the intensity of the moment, and plant the seeds of tomorrow.

ROCOCO AND ROMANTIC GARDENS

Gardens from early civilizations were adorned with all sorts of columns, statuary, and figurines—offerings, we can only assume, to the gods. As is the case with modern man, for early humanity gardens were a place to retreat from the travails of daily life as well as from invading hordes of conquering armies.

Realistically, it is possible to date and explore the use

of rustic architecture and furnishings through recent history. It appears that during the early part of the eighteenth century, wealthy landowners and gardening aficionados carefully structured their efforts according to the overbearing dogma and despotism of Louis XIV. After his death, an explosion of freedom and individualistic style emerged. Rococo

An antique Victorian photograph depicts a wonderful lakeside rustic structure and boathouse.

This rustic gazebo greets guests as they enter the historic Mohonk Mountain House in New York.

This postcard shows a rustic back porch of an inn that overlooks the Green Mountains of Vermont.

A local black bear is often seen, possibly enjoying the scenery, at this hidden gazebo located in the Catskill Mountains of central New York.

style and Romanticism, the premier movements of the day, were often described as exotic, light, eccentric, frivolous, and imaginative. These philosophies and movements filled lives with a renewed sense of passion, appreciation of nature, and a belief in the ideals of life.

DEFINING RUSTIC

Rustic furniture and architecture are chairs, tables, gazebos, pergolas, trellises, and other items influenced by and made to resemble nature. Rustic craftspeople utilize a variety of natural materials such as branches, sticks, roots, vines, twigs, and logs in their endeavors. Little or no attempt is made to disguise the materials. Often, the more extreme the knurls, burls, twists and curves inherent in the material, the better. Usually bark is left on the pieces. Rustic materials are not manipulated in the name of beauty. Rather, the more extreme in nature, the more unusual a piece may become.

From the beginning it should be mentioned that rustic furniture is, to some degree, a rebellion from tradition. It is a slap in the face to society. Its unsophisticated manner, in essence, is a departure from the norm. But equally important, rustic pieces offer a profound sense of humor. The gaiety and comedy natural to rustic furnishings is apparent to many on their first exposure to "rusticity."

But there is also a dark side to the realm of rustic. "Grotesque" is a term that often comes to mind. There is something almost "sick" inherent in the bumps and twists of nature. It's frightening to many, repulsive to a few, and sometimes downright ugly. Many of us sincerely hope that we, ourselves, never take on the warts and bumps often found on organic materials. We would find that quite disgusting, and yet these aberrations are forever a part of nature. Rustic furniture goes against convention. It is a state of disorder that suggests disunity, chaos, and anarchy with its presence. It is well outside of the organized world in which most of us live.

On the other hand, the organic nature of wood suggests freedom and knows no bounds. It contains sincere movement and often appears about ready to get up and dance. Certain personalities are drawn immediately to the essence of rustic furniture and garden architecture. Many find the passionate qualities enchanting. It brings them back to their roots. It rejuvenates and refreshes. It reminds onlookers of the natural world from which they emerged. But the freedom it symbolizes calls deeply to something inside most people. It is a call in an unspoken language. Most people hear it and are drawn to it almost out of need.

A delightful scenic gazebo sits precariously on the edge of a cliff, providing viewers with breathtaking scenery

A rustic walkway lined with numerous flower beds is located at the Mohonk Mountain House.

children and the occasional rendezvous of adults.

With the oppressive guidelines of Classicism lifted, creativity and self-expression flourished. Painters approached nature with a new emphasis on reality and ruggedness. Landscape architects sought a natural look, allowing nature to dictate the parameters of their landscape projects. Freedom abounded.

But other realities were in play. The parks and gardens were in essence country cathedrals, places of worship where worshippers could strive toward their ideals in life. Gardens at that time were sites to enhance cultural values and to focus on

Mid-Victorian garden structures and rustic chairs provided a quiet place to sit on hot summer afternoons.

THE NEW ENGLISH GARDEN

Bored with the symmetry of Louis XIV, English landscapers began to experiment with natural aberrations inherent on the garden site, following the natural contours of streams and hedges.

Gone was the enclosed look of high hedges. Gardens were opened up for the pleasures of passersby, and they began to include grottoes and hermitages—places for the secret meetings of

The meandering, quiet
gardens of the Mohonk
Mountain House.

A turn-of-the-century gazebo stands today as a monument to early rustic ingenuity in New York City.

individual spiritual needs.

No self-respecting garden, however, was without a grotto or hermitage. Seen as a primal symbol, these small dwellings dated back to the early Greeks, Romans, and Chinese. Traditionally, landowners did not live in such small shelters, but they retreated there for rest, contemplation, and commiseration with the gods of their times.

Initially, early religious fanatics and zealots sought refuge in caves for meditation. Metaphorically, these caves can be likened to openings in Mother Earth where one could return for security, safety, and contemplation. In time, cavelike structures, also

Thousands of wildflowers line the walkways of this estate where several inviting garden structures offer moments of rest for visitors and guests.

Probably one of the most elaborate structures ever built, this waterfront gazebo and bridge survived until the 1920s when it was torn down by the local village.

called grottoes, were prevalent in Roman gardens and were thought to be the home of Priapus, a local goddess of fertility.

Later, grottoes were lined with intricate mosaic patterns of shells, pebbles, and other shardlike materials.

Elaborate hydraulic apparatuses were invented for the entertainment and amusement of those lucky enough to afford such structures. Eventually, many of the grottoes were covered with bizarre designs and patterns. They became known as

This delicate gazebo is situated next to a Woodstock, New York, pond.

qualities. It was considered good luck to have a hermit residing in one's hermitage. So desirable was it, that local landowners would often advertise for social outcasts and hermits to reside free of charge in their shelters. If no responses occurred, then the landowners would hire local actors to pose as hermits for parties and special events. The presence of hermits, they believed, would bring good fortune and luck to those attending the many banquets and celebrations.

Much earlier in history the Chinese experimented with furniture of roots and sticks. Having made furniture from bamboo shoots for centuries, they were accustomed to natural materials. The Chinese and other oriental countries had also long experimented with the deliberate contortion of branches and roots of indigenous plants. These are commonly known today as bonsai plants, which are pruned and manipulated into forms felt sacred by gardeners. The artistic beauty of many bonsai plants as well as gardens from the Orient

grottoesque or, as we know it today, grotesque. They later became associated with demonic possessions and places that housed the evil spirits and the devil himself.

Hermitages, on the other hand, were often places of worship, and many had attached chapels for meditation and prayer. Apparently, they were first constructed under the direction of Philip II of Spain. Hermitages were usually constructed on the edges of gardens and were thought to house magical deities and maintain magical

This small mushroom-shaped
gazebo rests quietly between two
150-year-old white pines.

were–and are–quite awe inspiring and have motivated many gardeners around the world to incorporate oriental designs into their efforts.

Further, elaborate tea ceremonies and other pageantries were held in oriental garden houses commonly referred to as pagodas. With the advent of the tea and silk trade, oriental ideas and designs spread throughout the trading world of the time. Consequently, many gardens throughout Europe were suddenly the homes of oriental-influenced outdoor structures.

THE INFLUENCE OF THE INDUSTRIAL REVOLUTION

Around the early 1820s, during the first part of the Industrial Revolution, designers found a call for middle-class country cottages and second homes. *Les cottages ornée,* as they came to be known, were small garden structures that complemented secondary country homes of those who prospered because of emerging technology. These small garden structures were usually covered with vines and surrounded with a plethora of trees, shrubs, and flowers. Architects and designers did their best to have the structures appear as if they had grown from the exact spots where they were presently standing.

The ideology of escape from the torment of the inner city and low-tech industrial life was pervasive from the early 1800s to present day. This concept of escape from the big city to a simpler way of life was nothing new. It is a philosophy dating back to the Greeks and Egyptians. Simplicity, many philosophers argued, was better than complexity.

In America, the 1800s brought incredible industrial change. It also brought profound changes in lifestyles as well as decor. Gone were the musty and staid dictates of the overbearing dogma of Classicism. The Romanticists and Victorians loved nature. Carpeting, wallpaper, and furniture of all sorts were adorned with flowers, vines, leaves, and images of trees. Pottery, paintings, and textiles suddenly bore the spirit of nature at its finest.

Flowers were brought into the homes, and the art of the florist blossomed. Gardens were cultivated by individuals across the complete range of the social spectrum.

In the mid-1800s, landscape designer Andrew Jackson Downing forever changed the landscape of urban lifestyles in America. It was during this period that he designed and developed stylish homes for the middle and upper classes that blended well into natural surroundings within a stone's throw of the city. Serviced by railroads, suburbs sprang up all across the country and allowed individuals who

Aggressive vines took control of this gazebo in New York City.

This rustic gateway serves as an entrance to the Rustic Playground in Central Park.

Garden scene of a private
New York residence.

toiled in the city to take full advantage of the delights and naturalness of the country.

Not only did Downing profoundly influence the architecture of the day, but his meticulous plans for Central Park in New York City were carefully implemented by designer Frederick Law Olmstead. Unfortunately, Downing was killed in a tragic steamboat accident and was never able to complete the Central Park project. Fortunately, Olmstead was able to complete the project, and he went on using Downing's designs and ideas to complete parks and recreational landscaping across the country.

Central Park is considered the quintessential urban facility. Numerous gazebos, pergolas, trellises, and bridges, all in rustic design and constructed with natural materials, are placed throughout the park. Ponds, trees, sloping landscapes, open fields, rocky cliffs, and wonderful gardens offer New Yorkers a respite from the daily grind. Downing was careful to draw on the rustic influence of England, Switzerland, and the Black Forest region of Europe. Many of his designs are based on earlier rustic designs first developed in these regions and implemented throughout Europe and England. Downing's books *Cottage Residences*, 1842, and *The Architecture of Country Houses*, 1850, are still considered classic texts for rustic architecture and designs. Both books are liberally annotated with dozens of drawings of rustic architecture, including bridges, homes, and cottages.

Departing from the steps of a hidden gazebo, visitors wander out into the lush gardens of the Mohonk House.

Probably one of the most advanced Victorian gazebos still standing, the roof of its interior is completely mosaic inlay of hearts, flowers, and other romantic patterns.

The base of the Dakota
Hotel in Manhattan is the site
of a quiet gazebo scene in
Central Park.

A gazebo overlooking a scenic lake in the Catskills.

By the mid-1800s, many resorts from New York to Boston and including the Hudson Valley maintained gardens and rustic architecture. An entire school of art eventually developed in the Hudson Valley, and gazebos and other garden ornamentation were very popular in the Catskills and in the Woodstock, New York, area.

Eventually, of course, New Yorkers discovered the Adirondacks. It was there that the term rustic

A lakeside gazebo is not only a favorite spot for visitors, but also for birds who nest there in the spring.

A peaceful garden setting is also a favorite spot to feed horses on this estate in New York.

achieved its place in the history books. In the Adirondacks, architects catered to the whims of the financially fortunate by building structures so extraordinary that the expression "Adirondack Architecture" is now widely recognized even though the buildings are more than a hundred years old.

Realistically, the Swiss, Bavarians, and Scandinavians had been constructing rugged mountain structures for decades prior to the late 1800s. Usually made of logs,

A garden structure on an Adirondack lake. The use of full-grown logs often accentuates the feeling of being in the forest.

these structures seemed to offer continuity to the local forests. Eventually, American architects recognized the significance of chalet-style architecture and constructed homes in the Adirondacks influenced by these earlier European efforts.

With money often no object, architects such as William West Durant, William L. Coulter, William Distin, and Max Westhoff experimented with–much to the chagrin, pleasure, and approval of those paying the bills–a wide variety of rustic construction techniques. The notching of logs on log cabins, fireplaces, porches, staircases, fretwork, and many other architectural embellishments were advanced in terms of style, aesthetics, and complexity. It was, in reality, a period in time and place where the notion of organic structures achieved credibility and finally, at least in America, could be called an art form. Architects and builders wanted structures to blend with their surroundings. They were inspired by nature, and they wanted that inspiration

An antique rustic structure in the Adirondacks was used to greet an impressive number of guests as they arrived by boat for a weekend stay.

manifested in structures that appeared to grow right from the spot where they were constructing.

Of the private architectural wonders in the Adirondacks, none is finer in terms of rustic adoration than Camp Topridge on Upper St. Regis Lake. Owned by Marjorie Post of the Post and General Foods corporations, the camp is a spectacular wonder of organic architecture. Ben Muncil, a self-taught builder, and architect Theodore Blake devised plans for the

A small, rustic bridge along the Hudson River allows people to cross a stream that flows swiftly in the spring and almost dries up in late summer.

banisters; stunningly wild, organic log railings; intricately articulated fretwork and detailing on the boathouse and other areas; and the massive scale of the entire project. The facility, although having recently changed hands, is still privately held and stands as the finest example of Adirondack Architecture in North America.

It was during this period, just prior to and shortly after the turn of the century, that the term rustic made its most important advances into the lexicon and consciousness of the public in general. Rustic arbors, trellises, gazebos, and other garden architectural adorations flourished across the eastern coast of North America. All respectable parks and gardens had to have some kind of rustic garden architecture. Considering that individuals such as Alfred Vanderbilt, Marjorie Merriweather Post, J. P. Morgan, and several other prominent leaders in America had incredible rustic work on their estates, it

camp around 1920 and, according to legend, imported more than a hundred Norwegian loggers, carpenters, and craftsmen to complete the project, which included more than sixty-eight buildings. At full occupancy, the guests were catered to by a staff of eighty-five maids, cooks, guides, caretakers, butlers, personal servants, and more. But the real glory of the facility comes with its massive log

A mountain lookout gazebo at the Mohonk House in the Catskills.

Hanging ferns growing on an Adirondacks cliff ledge.

almost seemed appropriate for other financially aspiring individuals to maintain such rustic work as well.

FURTHER CONTRIBUTIONS

Unfortunately, the South had their own troubles during the Civil War, and many architectural jewels were lost because of the ravages of conflict and war. Almost immediately after the war, however, resorts began springing up throughout the wilderness regions of the South, including North Carolina, Tennessee, and Virginia. Most of the resort areas sprung up around hot springs, and spas across the area prospered.

Many of the early rustic architectural structures in the South were influenced by early English garden architecture. This, of course, was not surprising since the preponderance of southern settlers were of Scottish-Irish

This close-up of detail work by Romancing the Woods is from a structure that serves as a garden house and storage area for garden equipment.

These garden walkways are located at the base of Mohonk Mountain House in central New York.

For sheer delight, no gazebo offers a better view than this structure near Woodstock, New York.

Many gazebos turn
into delightful fantasy
shelters once they
become overgrown
with greenery.

descent. In time, however, southern craftsmen with names like E. L. Goodykoontz and Joseph Quinn made wild garden furniture from the roots and branches of rhododendron plants and also crafted interesting gazebos and other structures for spas in towns such as Hot Springs, Virginia; Sweet Springs, West Virginia; White Sulpher Springs, West Virginia; and Asheville, North Carolina.

Not surprisingly, conflicts bring strange bedfellows. During the First World War, many German soldiers were captured and interred in the town of Hot Springs, North Carolina. As the soldiers sat out the war years, they occupied their time applying their talents to the outdoor camps in which they were residing. There, they created some of the most incredible rustic community dwellings in the South. With no funds or materials supplied by the United States government, they constructed many small garden houses, cottages, gazebos, rustic fences, and rustic furniture of all shapes and sizes to meet the needs of more than two hundred prisoners. The builder's materials were fallen logs, bark from nearby trees, and used materials offered from the local townspeople.

The tiny town of Old Heidelberg sprang from the ashes of war and was the creative outlet for dozens of prisoners who could speak no English. Their homes were intricately decorated with rustic mosaic patterns of diamonds, trapezoids, triangles, stars, squares, and other creative geometric patterns. Very few tools were utilized by the builders. Observers were often amazed that the carpenters used only a few dull knives, axes, and saws, along with a mere handful of nails and just a few hammers among them to build an entire town that included a rustic two-story church with a towering steeple.

There is no doubt that the work of the prisoners was an influence on local folk artists and craftsmen. A talented lot, the Germans also established a band, using borrowed instruments from the local communities. On Sunday evenings they would practice different concerts, and people from far away would sit in picnic chairs just outside the prison fences, enjoying the music.

In short time, local spa owners recognized the inherent beauty of the prisoners' garden structures, and resorts throughout the countryside began constructing gazebos, mosaic garden houses, and other related rustic garden structures based on the German prisoners' efforts. Many believe the German influence was responsible for creating a significant interest in southern rustic garden architecture.

Other southern influences had to have come from the small city of Asheville, North Carolina. Two estates were built there that are so

This early postcard's photographer captured an intricate rustic structure found in the Adirondacks.

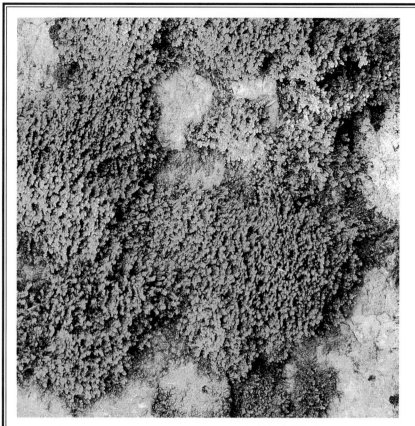

Natural beauty, such as this greenery, is often the inspiration of rustic builders.

amazing they both became national historic landmarks.

The Grove Park Inn opened its massive doors in July of 1913. Constructed of enormous boulders, the building is a stellar monument to human ingenuity. Lining the gigantic Grove Park porches were dozens of rustic rockers from the Old Hickory Chair Company in Martinsville, Indiana, and in the gardens were several rustic gazebos, trellises, and bridges that lined the pathways through forests of towering trees.

Another world-class structure in Asheville is the Biltmore House owned by George Vanderbilt. Constructed at the turn of the century, the Biltmore House can easily be considered one of the great estates of the world. Initially, hundreds of miles of woodlands, rolling hills, and sparkling streams made up the countryside of the estate, and the extraordinary gardens were filled with not only deer herds, swans, and other wildlife, but with rustic garden architecture as well. The Biltmore and the Grove Park Inn are alive and well today and are open for tours and accommodations. They are both still splendid; however, many of the original garden structures are unfortunately no longer standing.

For sheer presence and rustic majesty, no structure is more impressive, in terms of rustic garden architecture, than the Mohonk Mountain House in New Paltz, New York. First purchased by Albert Smiley in 1869, the facility underwent construction between 1879 and 1910. Today the magnificent mid- to late-Victorian structure offers 273 rooms in classical Victorian and Edwardian decor. Just outside the back doors is pristine Lake Mohonk surrounded by the majestic Shawangunk Mountains. Surrounding the complex is 21,000 acres of pristine mountain land, home to bear, deer, and mature forest.

Yet, for garden and rustic shelter lovers, nothing is more impressive than Mohonk. The inn presently

Hidden on a walkway at the Mohonk House is a sheltered gazebo surrounded by oak trees and acres of Queen Anne's lace.

An antique rustic structure in Connecticut.

offers 128 stunning gazebos, benches, fences, and garden arbors, many perched on cliff ledges, offering dramatic birds-eye views of the unspoiled area. Not to be forgotten are the spectacular gardens. Throughout the summer, flowers blossom into majestic celebrations with more color than one thought possible. Horses pull period carriages through the gardens, and guests can eat lunch on balconies overlooking the lake and mountains. It is a place left unchanged by time.

THE INHERENT BEAUTY OF RUSTIC WORK

Americans, being an entrepreneurial lot, came to recognize the inherent beauty and desirability of rustic work. Around the turn of the century, numerous commercial facilities jumped into the arena and offered structures of all sorts to garden-conscious individuals and communities around the country. At the turn of the century, the Old Hickory Chair Company of Martinsville, Indiana, made wonderful garden structures as well as a full range of rustic furnishings. Their pieces were constructed of hickory saplings recognized as the hardest and strongest wood in North America. The Old Hickory Chair Company was known for its superior workmanship and aesthetic designs. Several other companies around the country made garden furnishings and structures out of American red cedar. It is recognized as the preferred wood for outdoor structures because of its resistance to rot and insects.

Today, rustic garden architecture is enjoying considerable attention and rejuvenation. Several hundred individuals around the country enjoy constructing furnishings of a rustic nature and hundreds are able to make a decent living from their efforts. Several companies around the country—including Natural Edge owned by David Robinson of Pennington, New Jersey; Romancing the Woods of Catskill, New York; and others—offer high-quality rustic garden architecture that today is gracing the gardens, lawns, and landscapes of North America.

Rustic gazebos, chairs, pergolas, trellises, and benches came from—and blend with—nature. They increase the attractiveness and individuality of our yards and gardens, creating tranquil havens for growth and reflection. Simple, honest, enduring, and beautiful—rustic garden architecture is timeless.

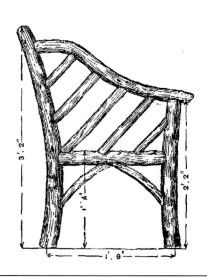

On a mountainside in the Catskills, this hidden gazebo and walkway reside.

Romancing the Woods created this charming and cozy garden gazebo.

A lovely, yet rugged,
rustic bridge.

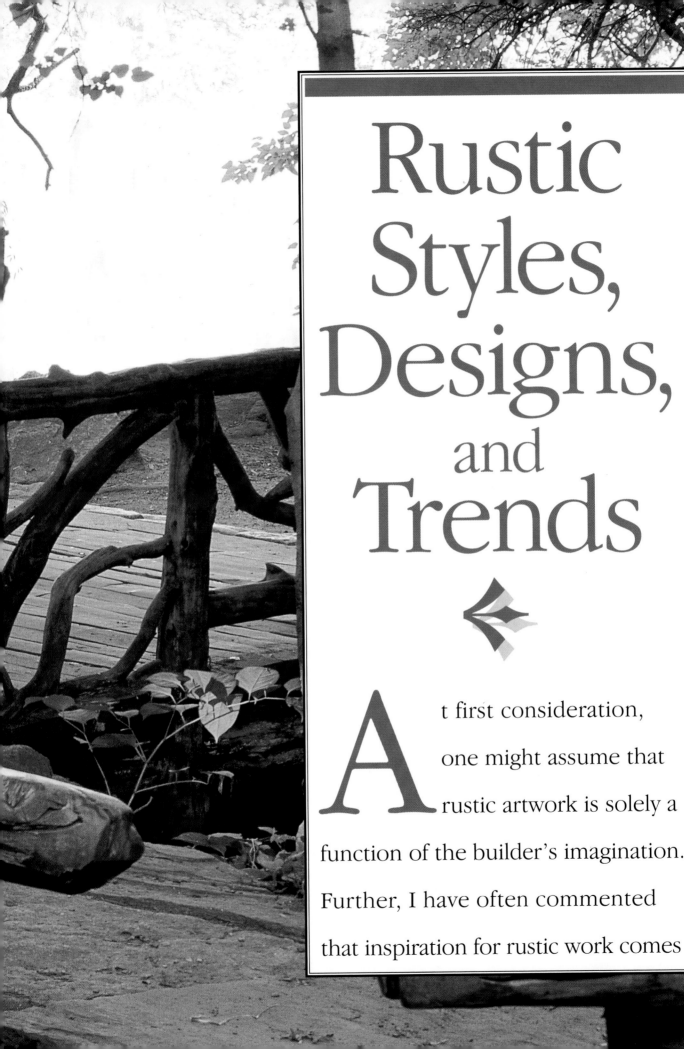

Rustic Styles, Designs, and Trends

A t first consideration, one might assume that rustic artwork is solely a function of the builder's imagination. Further, I have often commented that inspiration for rustic work comes mainly from nature. In essence, both of these comments are true. Nonetheless, varying styles do exist, and throughout

The intensity of scarlet flowers in late summer adds high drama to any rustic setting.

the years the influence of numerous trends and designs can be seen in the efforts of both historical and modern craftsmen.

Once the Orient opened its doors, the West was soon to adopt many trends from within that culture. Along with

paintings, architecture, culinary efforts, and other endeavors, furniture designs and related influences made their way into the decorative efforts of western builders. The latticework from the Orient quickly became popular,

Certainly one of the most profound rustic garden structures, this building in Poet's Walk Park will seat fifty people at once and is a favorite spot to watch the storms roll in from the west.

and Chinese Chippendale chairs are now a standard in the chair-design industry.

The oriental influence is prevalent within the rustic realm as well. At the turn of the century, several builders were making chairs, settees, and garden architectural ornamentations adorned with what certainly can be referred to as Chinese latticework. Heavily interwoven sticks were used to construct pergolas, gazebos, and the backs of many kinds of furnishings. It is a style that is commonly used today in all realms of rustic garden architecture.

Just after the turn of the century and under the influence of William Morris of Great Britain, Gustav Stickley and his brothers developed the Arts and Crafts or Mission movement here in America. Several years later, renowned architect Frank Lloyd Wright of Oak Park, Illinois, strongly influenced by Japanese architecture, introduced Prairie School designs to an adoring public. Both the Arts and Crafts and the Prairie School movements relied on heavily delineated lines; simple, timeless structure; and a working with, rather than against, nature. Both movements incorporated naturalness into their efforts, espoused simplicity, and shied away from excessive adoration and embellishments.

This gazebo resides near a private swimming pond, and swimmers often use the structure as a place to eat lunch or as shelter from the rain.

A uniquely
beautiful gazebo
by Romancing
the Woods

The natural freedom, boldness, and movement of roots often inspire artists.

Just prior to these movements, however, architects such as William Coulter incorporated intricate geometric stickwork on porches in the Adirondacks. Today, we refer to the intricate patterns often used on gazebos, porches, and related garden artwork as Mission or Prairie School influenced.

Another influence of equal importance is also prevalent in both historical and contemporary rustic garden furnishings and architecture. Throughout history, rustic builders extolled the message "let nature do the talking." Consequently, many rustic builders incorporate wildly organic elements into their structures. There is, of course, a profound sense of humor in this approach. Many structures have huge branches and logs artfully integrated into their framework. Builders have also incorporated roots and stumps from indigenous trees into structures and furnishings. This organic approach has met with passionate delight from many and has been frowned upon by others who feel that the organic approach is a bit too grotesque for their tastes. Nonetheless, it is art at its finest. At first glance, one may think that the incorporation of organic elements into furnishings and architectural structures is easy and can be completed with little effort. I can assure the reader, however, that it takes real craftsmanship and a profound artistic eye to integrate roots and trees into a sophisticated structure.

No matter what the style, rustic garden structures and furnishings are certain to please the eye, prompt an occasional chuckle, and blend beautifully with natural surroundings.

An organic lowland bridge by Jerry Farrell lies over a swamp and is used as a walkway for students wanting to observe swamp life up close.

This gazebo overlooks the massive stone house at Mohonk.

Gazebos

Garden gazebos have long been considered shelters for elves and druids. Homes of fantasy and frolic, they seem to grow from the ground upon which they're built. Gazebos are shelters for the young and the young in spirit. Romantic in nature, they suggest a passion all humans recognize.

Historic Victorian gazebo at a private residence in Lake George, New York.

One of only a few two-story gazebos in existence serves as a daily breakfast site for a couple in New York. It was initially eyed with concern by neighbors. Fortunately, they finally saw the light, and several added rustic gazebos to their properties as well.

This suggestiveness and romance linked to garden hideaways sings to the heart and the senses. The gnarled branches and twisted limbs lend themselves to an earthy sensuality.

Though garden gazebos bespeak passion and freedom, gardens, themselves, with all their freedoms and initiatives, are actually places of strict discipline and structure. Successful gardeners know what plants and colors complement each other. The most beautiful gardens are the result of careful planning and regimentation, contrary to the sense of freedom they allow human visitors.

Despite the discipline necessary for successful gardens, the act of gardening is, for many, a passionate act itself. Recently, as I sat sipping tea, visitor to an ivy-covered, rustic gazebo of an elderly woman friend, I sat spellbound as I listened to her talk about her garden. For more than seventy years she tended her plants. Each was her own great-great-great-grandchild seventy

This exceptionally well-made structure by David Robinson will last for decades and will always blend perfectly with the environment.

A picturesque gazebo on a private pond is an ideal spot for evening fishing and for relaxing while watching the sun set.

This stunning contemporary gazebo in Poet's Walk Park offers visitors not only an ideal place for lunch, but a tremendous view of the Hudson River as well.

A small red-cedar gazebo found at the Mohonk Mountain House is often used for small gatherings and afternoon tea.

This gazebo on the shores
of the Hudson River was built
by David Robinson.

An unusual structure,
this gazebo rests in a
garden shop just outside
Aspen, Colorado.

generations removed. As she told her tales, the tears swelled in her eyes. She told of the grief of losing her "children" each fall and the joy of their rebirth each spring. She would talk with each of them on a daily basis, and they would respond with their happy, blossoming faces. On rainy days she would serve tea in the gazebo, and although she had fewer visitors as the years took their toll, she still had her garden, which provided her endless delight and for which the gazebo was the focal point. She was never disappointed with her garden, believing with her tender care and direction

A wonderful gazebo by Romancing the Woods on a private estate. Modeling their structures on a variety of early Victorian designs, Romancing the Woods creates marvelous rustic garden architecture.

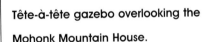

Tête-à-tête gazebo overlooking the Mohonk Mountain House.

that each plant would achieve its own potential.

Garden gazebos increase the quality of our lives. They offer rest and sanctuary. They give us a few minutes to reflect on our lives and ponder the great questions of the day. Their strange appeal often defies comprehension, and we can only acknowledge their unspoken calling with reverence, respect, and appreciation.

This rustic gazebo by David Robinson is certainly one of the finest examples of large garden structures, offering comfort to Central Park visitors in New York City.

Rustic Seating

Rustic settees and chairs stand as monuments to individuality and uniqueness. Cradles from the earth, their loving arms encompass us as only Mother Earth can, offering a peace and calmness that hi-tech chairs cannot. They blend in perfectly with a natural environment

A rustic settee serves as an ideal place for an afternoon picnic.

This Romancing the Woods' settee on a private estate will probably last for decades.

and age gracefully to the warm tones of the earth. As I have often experienced, rustic chairs and settees actually seem to smile at me. They are friendly and inviting, welcoming and even encouraging sitters to experience their presence. Their infectious humor sometimes leaves me smiling to myself, giving me a sense of connection to all living things. Rustic settees, chairs, and rockers, however, provide more than just rest. They offer relaxation and communion with nature; they offer a chance to feel the textures of things natural, and they offer humor, providing the opportunity to ignore the dictates of our complex world. Yet, rustic seating is not always comfortable. Rumor has it that Winslow Homer had a pair of very uncomfortable chairs on the back porch of his Adirondack vacation home.

A pair of settees by David Robinson of Trenton, New Jersey.

A rustic settee by Romancing the Woods demonstrates creative design patterns in the back. Designs are limited only by the imaginations of the builders.

Probably one of the most original settees ever constructed, this half-round settee by David Robinson is often used for storytelling in the evenings.

When unwanted visitors came around, he would always seat them in these uncomfortable chairs. Within ten minutes the gnarls and knots would get to them, and they would politely excuse themselves and depart. This idea does have its merits. Several years ago, I was asked to design a number of chairs for a Rocky Mountain theme park. The owners did not want their clients sitting too long, so I

An organic settee and
garden house in
Saugerties, New York.

A settee by Romancing the Woods is placed on a stone terrace that also serves as a barbecue station for an estate.

An afternoon picnic in a rustic setting.

reversed the angle of the seats on the chairs, and within ten minutes of sitting, the customers went off to spend more money. Needless to say, the owner of the facility was delighted. (I must admit that I did not want my name associated with the chairs, and to this date I have a hard time admitting to myself that I designed them.) Rustic furnishings are art and nature incarnate. In addition, rustic chairs have an attitude. They seem to say, "I don't care," existing outside of mainstream society, and for a few seconds that allows us to do the same. Their humor is unmistakable. Their dark side reminds us of how vulnerable we all are, and, once in a great while, they remind us that we are, in reality, a part of the earth ourselves. They dispel our fears and renew our fascination and

This settee is situated along a trail in central New York's Poet's Walk Park.

wonderment with the marvels of nature. Rustic chairs and settees are the thrones of the gods.

A late Victorian garden bench is often used as a resting site for visitors along a trail in the rocky areas of central New York.

Hidden in the woods,
this settee by Romancing
the Woods offers a chance
for rest in all seasons.

A walkway at Bushart Gardens
in Vancouver.

Rustic Garden Architecture

RUSTIC PERGOLAS AND TRELLISES

Wisteria, trumpet vine, climbing roses, honeysuckle, grapes, morning glory, and many other climbing plants have inspired builders for generations to attempt to accommodate their upward growth. Rustic supports are not only

picturesque, they blend naturally with the garden rather than competing with the vine for the viewer's attention.

Given the opportunity, vines will ascend any-thing above themselves, including the local telephone pole. In one instance, an upstate New York power company strung a new line of poles several years ago. Within two years, the last three poles were completely vine covered, blending beautifully with the terrain. Unfortunately, the power company failed to see the inherent value and humor of the vines and, with great effort, removed them from the poles. Not to be outdone or defeated by mere humans, the vines refused to suffer the indignities of human efforts to destroy them, and by the following year they had reascended nearly half of the pole.

Certainly one of the beauties of plant aggressiveness is that they can be sculptured into almost any form or shape we desire. If we want a little shade, we can plant a few trees, and twenty years later we'll have shade. On the other hand, if we want shade within a few years, we can build a pergola and plant any number of climbing vines that will

This detail shot is from a structure by David Robinson that stands in Poet's Walk Park. The structure will be completely vine covered in a few years.

This new structure was recently placed near a pool in central New York. The owners have planted several climbing vines, and within a few years the structure should be covered with plants, including some that will attract hummingbirds.

The entrance to Poet's Walk Park in New York City is a massive red-cedar pergola built by David Robinson of Trenton, New Jersey.

The Secret Gardens at New York's Central Park.

A small rustic structure created by Romancing the Woods.

provide shelter from the sun, a place for afternoon tea, or a covered walkway.

Trellises, on the other hand, are usually two-dimensional, ornamental structures of varying sizes erected by landscapers and gardeners who allow climbing plants to ascend at their discretion. Both trellises and gazebos are ideal for creating walls and barriers as well as providing homes for flowers of unbelievable beauty.

Whether it be ivy or wisteria or grape vines they support, rustic pergolas and trellises add beauty and shade to any garden setting.

Trellis work found at the Bushart Gardens on Vancouver Island.

This pergola is hidden by mature growth of vines and hanging plants. The interior of the structure is used for Sunday morning coffee and newspaper reading.

Hydrangeas and tiger lilies
occupy water's edge on a
quiet pond, a beautiful
view from a rustic settee
or gazebo.

An antique rustic gazebo, almost completely obscured by greenery, is accessible by a small path large enough for children only. They use the gazebo as a clubhouse and play area. No grown-ups allowed!

Massive log pillars support the front porch of a great camp in the Adirondacks.

Nature on the Porch

Every once in a while, people become inspired by the wonderful forces of nature–the naturally occurring knurls, twists, burls, and bumps of a tree. Certainly, humans would be limiting themselves if they thought that nature

Ferns create beautiful backdrops in shaded areas.

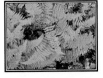

The back porch of this Adirondack great camp was designed by William Coulter in the early part of the 1900s.

Rather than stripping the bark off eastern red cedar, Romancing the Woods prefers the classical look of retained bark on their structures. This porch was added to a contemporary home, lending an element of nature.

belonged only in gardens. Many realize nature can play a greater part in their lives, and they extend natural influences into their homes. The results are log homes, which today are often marvels of high technology, grace, and charm.

Fortunately, numerous creative people around the country often look at the inherent humor in all the bumps, twists, and curves on natural trees and decide to incorporate some of the fun into their homes. Realistically, there are several different modes, forms, or styles of this sort of decoration.

In the West, lodgepole pines are known to react

A 1980s house in the Catskills is made far more interesting by the addition of rustic porches and fences.

These geometric patterns for a back porch were created by an architect at the turn of the century. The cottage overlooks a spectacular lake in the Adirondacks.

violently to insect bites and injuries. They have a tendency to wildly contort and grow huge burls around their injuries, much the same way people grow scabs and scars. Many builders take advantage of, as well as great delight in, this tendency and often adorn their porches, banisters, railings, and other architectural elements with aberrated wood. Several facilities, including the Old Faithful Inn in Yellowstone Park and the Million Dollar Cowboy Bar in Jackson, Wyoming, have incorporated idiosyncratic woods, and they are marvels of stunning architecture because of their uniqueness.

In the Adirondacks, many of the earlier turn-of-the-century homes had their porches decorated with straight-cut cedar poles. Several of these porches were filled with intricate geometric patterns of trapezoids, diamonds, rectangles, and squares. William Coulter, a well-known Adirondack architect who completed numerous great camps in the Saranac Lake, New York, area, was known to adorn his porches

with a variety of patterns. Some contemporary builders have adapted this style and today are completing porches, gazebos, and other related structures based on the designs and styles of their predecessors.

During what I refer to as the Modern Era of Rustic Design, several builders today are incorporating organic rustic ideas into their efforts. Certainly, many of these builders are concentrating on the tremendous curves often inherent in organic materials. It is not uncommon to see porches and staircases with massive curled branches as banisters

and railings. This style can certainly be referred to as organic in nature.

Most rustic builders are very capable of constructing unique architectural adorations and embellishments, so those considering adding on to their houses or porches should mention to their contractors that they would like a rustic addition to their homes. If the contractor is unable or unwilling to comply, a local rustic builder may be able to create something natural and unique. For those interested, a list of exceptional builders is provided in the back of this book.

Lilies and grasses are easily managed by local gardeners and offer a rich, aesthetically pleasing background for rustic shelters.

A garden setting with white and pink cleome.

Master rustic builder Lionel Maurier enjoys his creation of an apple-tree settee.

Building
and
Preserving
Rustic
Structures

I will be the first to admit that I am not a rustic-furniture maker. I don't have the patience for it. Still, for the past twenty years, I have been closely involved in designing and producing

Working on a dome for the top of a gazebo.

rustic furniture and structures of almost any type imaginable. I have also been fortunate to see what does and does not hold up. The suggestions below have been culled from the knowledge and experience of many professional builders around the country.

Actually, it's easy to make rustic furniture. At my gallery in Lake George, New York, I have people coming by daily, offering me their latest creations. Many pieces are exceptional–most are not. One individual used twine to tie a number of sticks together then offered me, at great expense, his rustic chairs and tables. The chairs were very loose, and the tables were wobbly. When confronted with these flaws, he told me to untie the rope and tie the knots tighter. To this day, I'm certain he has never sold

Roots of a hardwood tree seem to flow over the ground and are often inspirational to rustic builders.

anything. The point is that quality sells and quality lasts. Mediocre furniture falls apart quickly. Quality, in itself, is art.

Making exceptional, high-quality rustic furniture and structures is, at best, time consuming and difficult. It takes craftsmanship, years of experience, patience, and a profound love of the craft to make high-quality rustic furniture. Inspiration for making rustic furniture does not come from the workshop or from books. I have had this conversation many times with the best builders in the country, and every one of them, without prompting from myself, freely admits that inspiration comes from walking in the woods and allowing nature to dictate, to inspire, to speak clearly what needs to be done. This is not an exaggeration. The most-respected artists in the business, including Barry

The gardens at Mohonk.

Drilling screw holes for a gazebo.
Screws are used instead of nails
because screws can be tightened
in years to come.

Gregson, Barney Bellinger, Clifton Monteith, Jerry Farrell, Brent McGregor, Phil Clausen, Lionel Maurier, and several others are very clear on this, suggesting builders spend time in the woods to discover what nature can tell them.

Most good rustic-furniture makers are extraordinarily friendly and open with their information. In my other books, I have included lengthy lists of rustic-furniture makers from around the country. Don't hesitate to call any of them and ask for building tips. However, a word of caution. The established builders do this for a living and almost all of them are successful because they have developed, after years of effort and expense, their own designs and styles. One of the most accomplished builders in the country lives near me in the Adirondacks. Throughout the years, he has had more than five hundred aspiring rustic-furniture makers visit him and his workshop because he has long been recognized as an excellent mentor in the business. Unfortunately, a number of entry-level people have started making exact copies of his work. More unfortunate is the fact that because of this imitation, the builder is no longer accepting visitors.

Finding a person's own style is important. It identifies the maker and offers a contribution to the artistic world as a whole. So, my suggestion is to create a unique style and avoid copying the works of others.

THE BASICS

An apple-tree settee is an excellent starting piece. Apple is a high-quality wood of dense grain and it has a wonderful sense of organic

A detail shot of a garden setting.

A newly constructed rustic settee finds a home in a New Hampshire strawberry patch.

freedom. Like other woods, it will twist and contort itself into all sorts of shapes and sizes for access to the sun, and it is plentiful because many years ago, Johnny Appleseed planted thousands of apple trees all around the country.

Once a year, gardeners and farmers at apple orchards prune their trees and cut away hundreds of medium- to large-size branches. These branches

A pile of freshly cut apple wood will become a variety of chairs, settees, and tables.

are either discarded or turned into firewood. Fortunately, orchard keepers will happily sell you piles of this wonderful material for just a few dollars. So, make a deal with your local orchard and load up your truck. Usually, you can count on using only about 10% of the wood you collect, so don't be afraid to accumulate a significant amount.

Once you get home, trim the branches and stack the wood neatly near your workshop so your spouse and/or neighbors won't complain. Make sure you stack the

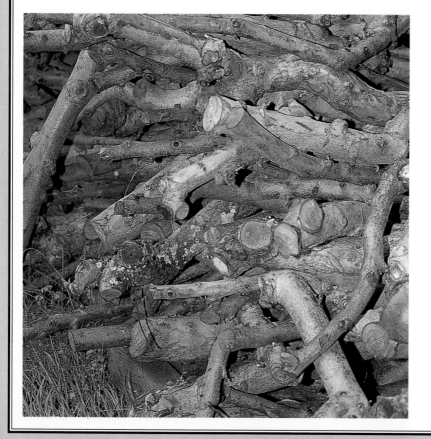

wood off the ground on old two-by-fours to prevent contact with the ground, thus avoiding wood rot. About six months later, the bark will naturally loosen and, with a little help, will fall to the ground.

BUILDING A SETTEE

More than anything else, excluding sturdiness and art, you want a reasonable semblance of comfort in furniture. Frank Lloyd Wright often said that the most difficult thing he ever designed were chairs. "They were so difficult to make comfortable," he often complained. The secret to comfortable chairs lies in the correct tilt or lean of the back. Since it's nearly impossible to bend thick apple branches, you have to find some that naturally arch. So, go through your woodpile and find two heavy legs that have a similar bend. They should be about forty-eight inches long. These are the back legs. Next, find another heavy pair for the front legs, about the same diameter–four inches–and about twenty-eight inches long.

An employee of Romancing the
Woods chisels off a few unwanted
knobs and bumps.

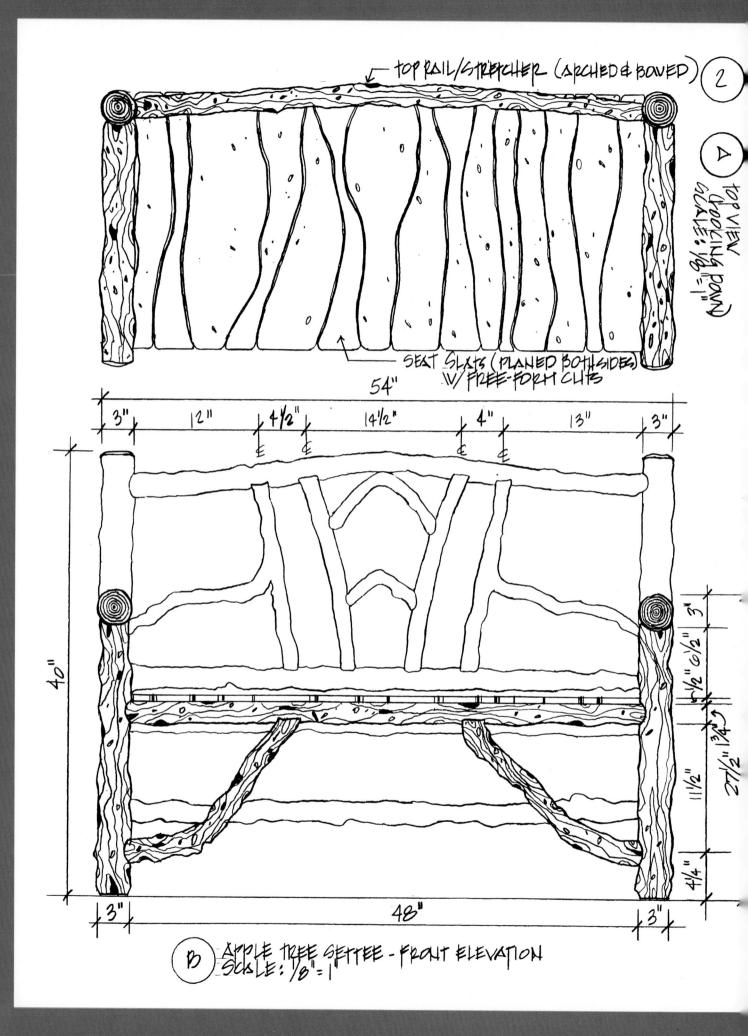

TOP RAIL/STRETCHER (ARCHED & BOWED)

② Ⓐ TOP VIEW (LOOKING DOWN) SCALE: 1/8" = 1'

SEAT SLATS (PLANED BOTH SIDES) W/ FREE-FORM CUTS

54"

3" | 12" | 4½" | 14½" | 4" | 13" | 3"

40"

3"

6½" | 6½"

2½" | 2¾"

11 | 1½"

4¼"

3" | 48" | 3"

Ⓑ APPLE TREE SETTEE - FRONT ELEVATION SCALE: 1/8" = 1'

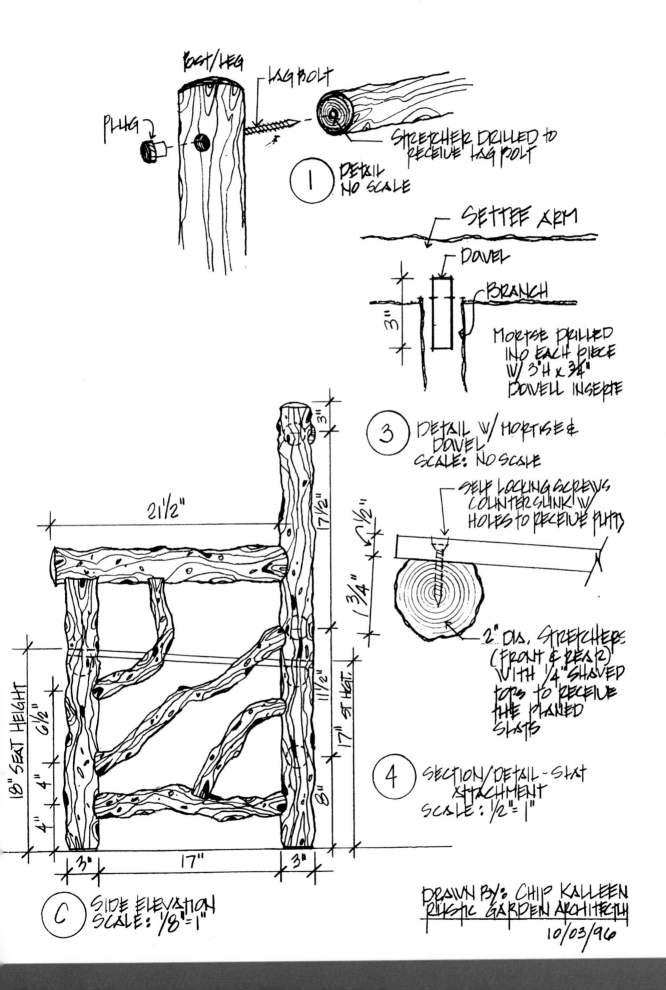

POST/LEG

LAG BOLT

PLUG

STRETCHER DRILLED TO RECEIVE LAG BOLT

1 DETAIL
NO SCALE

SETTEE ARM

DOVEL

BRANCH

3"

MORTSE DRILLED INO EACH PIECE W/ 3"H x 3/4" DOVELL INSERTE

3 DETAIL W/ MORTISE & DOVEL
SCALE: NO SCALE

21 1/2"

3"

17 1/2"

6 1/2"

18" SEAT HEIGHT

4"

4"

3"

17"

3"

SELF LOCKING SCREWS COUNTERSUNK W/ HOLES TO RECEIVE PLUG

1/2"

3/4"

11 1/2"

17" ST. HGT.

8"

2" DIA. STRETCHERS (FRONT & REAR) WITH 1/4" SHAVED TOPS TO RECEIVE THE PLANED SLATS

4 SECTION/DETAIL-SLAT ATTACHMENT
SCALE: 1/2"=1"

C SIDE ELEVATION
SCALE: 1/8"=1"

DRAWN BY: CHIP KALLEEN
RUSTIC GARDEN ARCHITECTURE
10/03/96

A palm sander smooths the edges of a settee.

Using a drawknife as another method to smooth out the edges on an apple-tree settee.

You are making a copy of the apple settee pictured above. Although I've already made my argument against copying the works of others, for the sake of this chapter and the learning process, we'll follow the dimensions of the settee and the construction techniques involved.

Now, pick out four straight logs–two about seventy inches long and two about twenty-two inches long. These are the stretchers that will connect all the legs. If you want your logs peeled or stripped of bark, make sure this is done before you attempt assembling the settee.

At this point, you're ready for the fun part. Once you've picked out your logs for the legs and the four branches for the stretchers, you have to consider a method of joining them. The simplest way, of course, is to take a few nails and bang the piece together. Or, you may wish to take four lag bolts and

Drilling screw holes for the gingerbread work on a settee. Great care and thought must be given to placement to ensure artistic and craftsmanship quality.

Cutting slats that will become the seat of the settee.

screw the different parts into place. Both processes are easy but in the long run prove to be ineffective methods of joinery.

The way the apple settee was joined is a bit more complicated. Make sure that each of the four stretchers is scribed and a concave groove is cut to fit perfectly into the diameter of the adjoining leg. The concave groove, or rounded end of the stick, can be cut with a band saw. Drill a hole, or mortise, completely through the back side of the adjoining leg and countersink it deep enough to hide the bolt. Cut a small dowel to cover the lag-bolt hole. Thus, the joint will fit snugly and tightly. This method should be used on each of the principal joints. It is a method of lag-bolt joinery widely used among builders because if the wood shrinks further than it already has, the bolts can be tightened to sturdy up the piece.

Using a wooden mallet to adjust the back brace on a settee. A wooden mallet is used as a hammer because a metal hammer would scar the wood.

Pre-drilling a hole to secure fretwork for the back of a settee.

The top rail supporting the back is crucial. Make sure there is a slight curve in the branch before setting it in place. While allowing for slight arch in the back legs, make sure the top arch bows away from the seat. This will ensure a comfortable settee. Join the top rail exactly as you did the posts and stretchers.

The fretwork, or gingerbread adorations, is the most fun to create. I personally prefer an intense look with many branches going every which way. Other people prefer a more monastic, simple look with just a few artistically placed branches to fill the voids. No matter what your preference, com-

fort is important here. Before you permanently affix the gingerbread, stop and consider both the comfort and artistic values. Don't just add something to fill a hole. Look at the piece and get a feel for its values. Let the piece do the talking. Let it inspire you. Great art makes you feel. Make sure it

This garden setting is located at a rustic site in the Catskill Mountains.

feels right before you proceed. Nature is full of movement. Let it dance and be itself. Don't just place an element piece because you want the project completed. Let it really sing, and don't finish it until the piece says it's finished. These may seem like strange thoughts, but great art has to make a statement. Make it wonderful. Make it fun. Let it be rebellious. Let it speak of freedom. Let it be part of yourself.

A number of ways to attach the gingerbread are also available. Once again, you can just take some nails and finish the piece. The apple settee, however, was joined by drilling a mortise into both the central post and the adjoining branch. A dowel was carefully fitted into each, and the piece was glued after the joint was carefully scribed to assure a custom fit. Minor joinery is completed by pre-drilling holes into both primary and secondary pieces, applying a small amount of wood glue to the pre-drilled joint, and joining the piece with finish nails. Pre-drilling ensures

that the ends of the small branches don't split.

Rustic-furniture seats are often completed with wood slats. Often, the front and rear stretchers are planed level with a power planer or by hand with a rasp or plane. Slats are then planed level on two sides to assure a level seat. Next, the slats are carefully fitted and fixed with self-locking screws, countersunk, and the holes are covered with wood putty. When completing a seat, make sure to leave just a small amount of room between the slats to

allow for moisture to seep through in case something is spilled on the piece.

FINISHES

Before we talk about finishes, you should be perfectly clear about the nature of wood. Wood, simple as it seems, is an organic product. In time, if left outdoors, all wood returns to the soil. Some woods last longer than others, but, Mother Earth calls, and sooner or later all wood will decompose. Having sold rustic furniture for the past twenty years,

This David Robinson settee is found in Llewlen Park, New Jersey—the home of numerous Robinson settees and structures. Residents delight in the ambiance added by the structures.

I have seen numerous pieces left outdoors that fall apart within a few years. Moisture, bugs, and funguses contribute to the deterioration of wood. I tell every one of my rustic-furniture buyers to keep the pieces on a covered porch and out of the way of moisture. I also mention that pieces should be rubbed down with tung oil or another finish once a year. This will kill any little creatures, such as powderpost beetles, living on the wood and add a few years of life to the patina of the piece.

Certain wood reacts differently to the elements than other woods. For instance, redwood has been known to survive quite well in the elements. However, eastern red cedar is probably more resistant to the elements than any other wood. Consequently, almost all of the outdoor structures being constructed today are of red cedar. Cedar has numerous toxins–not for humans–that repel bugs and smell delightful. It has been known to last for generations outdoors and is ideal for outdoor rustic garden structures.

A gazebo overlooking the massive structure of the Mohonk Mountain House is one of more than two hundred such structures found at this historic site in New Paltz, New York.

To withstand the elements, other woods require different treatment, and each rustic builder has his or her own opinion about finishes. Many prefer polyurethane, some like satin lacquer, some prefer acrylic finishes, others choose tung oil, and others still prefer a combination of boiled linseed oil and turpentine in a fifty-fifty mix. For outdoor treatment, many builders today are using spar varnish–a marine finish that is quite resistant to moisture, insects, fungus, and nasty molds of all sorts. Some

In time, rustic structures, including this rustic cedar bridge, blend in perfectly with their immediate environments.

One of many rustic garden structures at Old Orchard Park in Massachusetts, which opened in 1866.

builders prefer to apply finishes with a brush, and others find the practicality of spraying on a finish significantly easier. When applying products like tung oil, it's probably easier just to use a rag as a paintbrush. At any rate, you should experiment with a variety of different products and application techniques to discover which one you like best. I should mention that the apple-tree settee was finished with three coats of spar varnish applied with a brush. If you're going to leave a piece outside, make sure you finish the bottoms of the legs to prevent moisture from creeping up them. You may also want to place the legs on small cement blocks or pressure-treated wood placed in the ground. Do as much as you can to prevent moisture from coming in direct contact with the wood.

ANTIQUES AND FLEA-MARKET FINDS

Every once in a while, we may acquire a piece of outdoor furniture at a flea market or yard sale that has been left out in the elements. Often, these pieces have turned completely gray. Usually, they can be saved if the majority of wood is still solid. If the piece is wobbly, it may just be a matter of knocking apart all the joints, then regluing and replacing all the nails that were removed to undo the piece. Once you reglue a chair, however, make sure you find a level spot, sit in the chair to assure that it is level, then replace the nails or screws.

If the chair has lost its color, it's easy to replace patina. I often take a bucket of soap and water and wash the chair completely. Make sure that all the soap has been removed once the chair is clean. To return color or to lighten the piece, liberally apply some sort of deck cleaner. Leave the chair in the sun for several minutes, then thoroughly rinse the chair, using a garden hose. Make sure you remove all the cleaner because it may play havoc once you reapply a finish. In years past, we used oxcilic acid or Clorox bleach to lighten a gray chair. It's easier today to purchase a professional wood cleaner from the local hardware store. Just make sure you thoroughly rinse the chair when finished.

Once the chair is dry, you can either color the piece with any color stain you choose or you can apply any of the finishes mentioned above. Don't forget to sand the chair between coats.

A wonderful garden gazebo by Romancing the Woods in Woodstock, New York. The setting is a private lake in central New York.

source list

BRENT MCGREGOR
P.O. BOX 1477
SISTERS, OR 97759
541-549-1322

Brent is an exceptional rustic-furniture maker who also builds extraordinary staircasings, banisters, railings, and other rustic embellishments. He has also been known to place huge trees in home interiors. Brent works in the western style.

OLD HICKORY FURNITURE
COMPANY
403 SOUTH NOBLE STREET
SHELBYVILLE, IN 46176
800-232-2275

The Old Hickory Furniture Company has been creating high-quality rustic hickory furniture for more than a century. Makers there also build well-made rustic garden architecture.

DAVID ROBINSON
NATURAL EDGE
515 TUXFORD COURT
TRENTON, NJ 08638
609-737-8996

David is widely regarded as one of the premier garden architectural builders in the country. His gazebos are professionally constructed, and his rustic furniture, including settees, chairs, and tables, are not only comfortable but artistically pleasing, too.

KEN HEITZBOX
161, ROUTE 28
INDIAN LAKE, NY 12412
518-251-3327

Ken has been in the rustic-furniture business for the past twenty years. He produces a wide variety of settees, railings, and related rustic furnishings.

JAKE LEMON
P.O. BOX 2404
SUN VALLEY, ID 83353
208-788-3004

Jake produces a wide variety of rustic furnishings and related architectural elements.

LIONEL MAURIER
26 TUCKER MOUNTAIN ROAD
MEREDITH, NH 03253
603-279-4320

Lionel is the consummate rustic builder. He has personally constructed more than fifty full-size log homes as well as numerous gazebos, settees, porches, and related elements.

CLIFTON MONTEITH
P.O. BOX 9
LAKE ANN, MI 49650
616-275-6560

Clifton is also widely regarded as one of the premier rustic builders in the country. He builds with a large selection of woods, and he has made many rustic chairs, settees, full-size porches, and other elements.

This western red-cedar gazebo was built in the Aspen, Colorado, town square.

ROMANCING THE WOODS
MARVIN DAVIS AND BOB O'LEARY
33 RAYCLIFFE DRIVE
WOODSTOCK, NY 12498
914-246-6976

Romancing the Woods constructs a variety of rustic elements, including garden bridges, gazebos, settees, and other furnishings. Their pieces are both exceptionally well made and aesthetically pleasing.

FRANK HAMM
341 BEACON STREET #3E
BOSTON, MA 02116
617-899-5752
OR 617-236-1086

Frank is certainly one of the more advanced builders on the East Coast. He builds a broad range of rustic furnishings as well as some extraordinary railings, banisters, porches, and related garden architecture.

JUDD WEISBERG
ROUTE 42
LEXINGTON, NY 12452
518-989-6583

Judd is one of the longtime builders on the East Coast. He builds not only wonderful rustic garden structures, but exceptional interior and exterior rustic furniture as well.

BARRY GREGSON
CHARLEY HILL ROAD
BOX 88
SCHROON LAKE, NY 12870
518-532-9384

Barry is best known for his extraordinary lilac tables and chairs. He does, however, build high-quality settees, railings, banisters, and porches as well. Be sure to visit him at his gallery in the Adirondacks.

RON FIELDS
SHASTA STIX
400 NORTH WASHINGTON DRIVE
MT. SHASTA, CA 96067
916-235-2105

Ron builds a wide range of rustic furnishings. His furnishings are well constructed, functional, and comfortable.

KUDZU
P.O. BOX 2277
NEW LONDON, CT 06320
800-W.V. ROOTS

The folks at Kudzu make rustic furnishings out of rhododendron and mountain laurel roots and branches. Their furniture is unique and offers a profound rustic flavor to any setting.

BURLS BY BURLEIGH
GLENN BURLEIGH
P.O. BOX 106
POWELL BUTTE, OR 97753
541-548-6913

Glenn builds some of the most unusual rustic furniture in the West. Built mostly of twisted juniper, his furniture offers both humor and fantasy.

JERRY FARRELL
P.O. BOX 225
SIDNEY CENTER, NY 13839
607-369-4916

Jerry is regarded by many as one of the most remarkable rustic builders in the country. His expertise includes probably the best mosaic work in the country, root furniture, and a wide array of rustic garden architecture.

CAMP RUSTIX
P.O. BOX 6190
41578 BIG BEAR BOULEVARD
BIG BEAR LAKE, CA 92315
909-866-2900

The folks at Camp Rustix build quality handcrafted log furniture and railings.

HIGH COUNTRY DESIGN
P.O. BOX 5348
BRECKEN RIDGE, CO 80424
970-468-1107

High Country Design creates attractive stick furniture and accessories along with a wide array of other rustic items.

This rustic structure, situated next to a mountain path, was made of eastern red cedar.

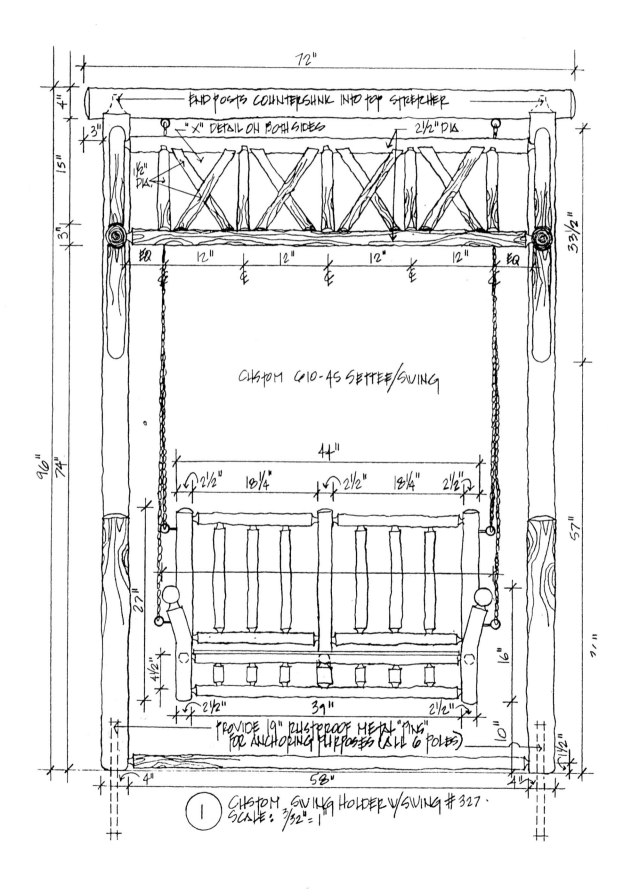

72"

4"

END POSTS COUNTERSHNK INTO TOP STRETCHER

3"

"X" DETAIL ON BOTH SIDES   2½" DIA

15"

½"
DIA

33½"

3"

EQ   12"   12"   12"   12"   EQ

CUSTOM 610-45 SETTEE/SWING

96" 74"

44"

2½"   18¼"   2½"   18¼"   2½"

57"   7'1"

27"

16"

4½"

2½"   39"   2½"

10"

PROVIDE 19" RUSTPROOF METAL "PINS"
FOR ANCHORING PURPOSES (ALL 6 POLES)

1½"

4"   58"   4"

① CUSTOM SWING HOLDER W/SWING #327.
   SCALE: 3/32" = 1"

GA-1165
8/9/94 C.K.

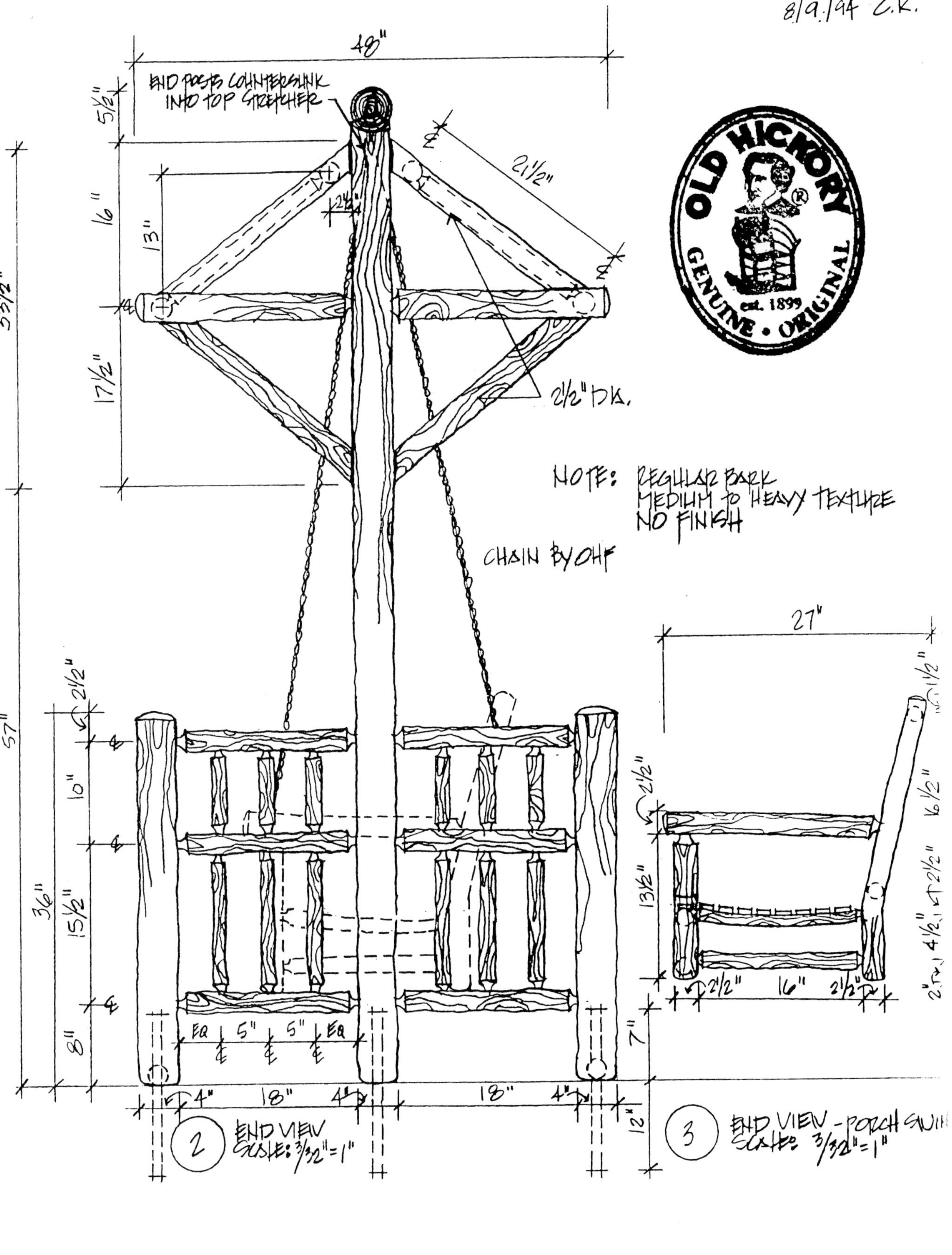

18"

END POSTS COUNTERSUNK
INTO TOP STRETCHER

5½"
16"
13"
21½"

33½"

17½"

2½" DK.

OLD HICKORY
GENUINE · ORIGINAL
est. 1899

NOTE: REGULAR BARK
MEDIUM to HEAVY TEXTURE
NO FINISH

CHAIN BY OHF

27"

1½"

57"

2½"

10"

2½"

13½"

36"

15½"

16½"

4½"

2½"

8"

7"

EQ   5"   5"   EQ

2½"   16"   2½"

4"   18"   4½"   18"   4"

12"

2   END VIEW
SCALE: 3/32"=1"

3   END VIEW - PORCH SWING
SCALE: 3/32"=1"

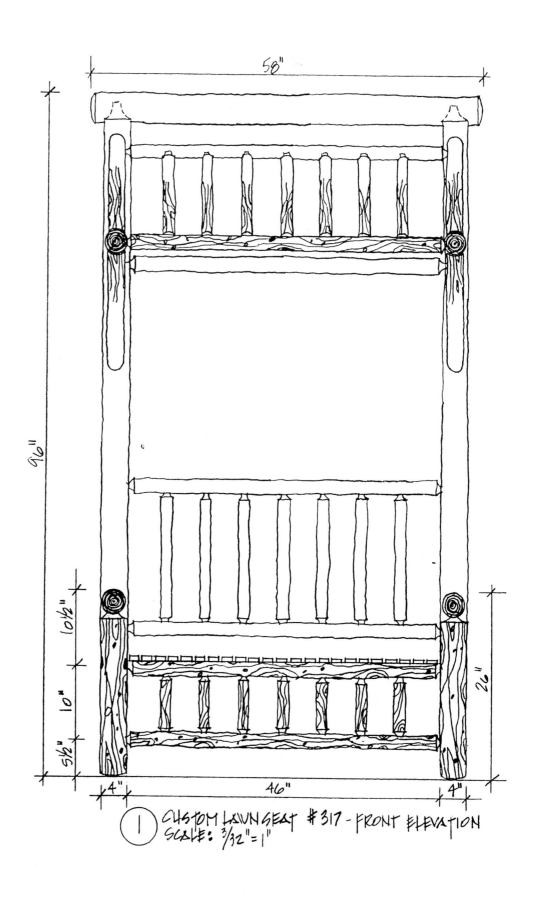

58"

96"

10½"

10"

5½"

26"

4"   46"   4"

① CUSTOM LAWN SEAT #317 - FRONT ELEVATION
  SCALE: ³/₃₂" = 1"

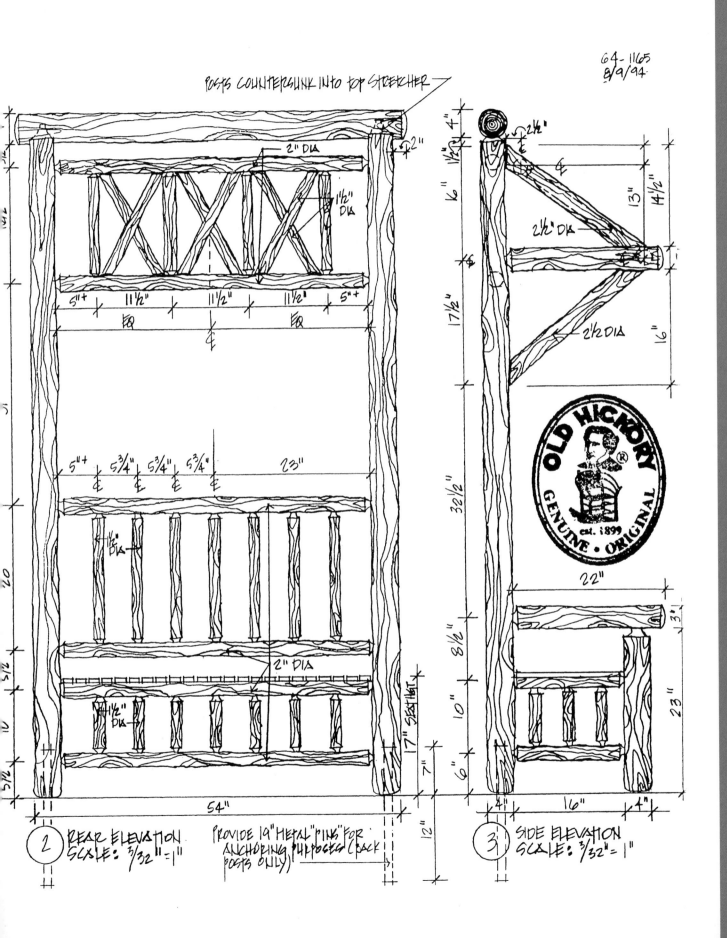

POSTS COUNTERSUNK INTO TOP STRETCHER

64-1165
8/9/94

2" DIA

1½" DIA

5"+   11½"   11½"   11½"   5"+
EQ   EQ

5"+ 5¾" 5¾" 5¾"   23"

1½" DIA

2" DIA

1½" DIA

7" SEAT HGT

2½" DIA

13"

14½"

2½" DIA

2½" DIA

16"

OLD HICKORY
GENUINE · ORIGINAL
est. 1899
®

22"

3"

23"

2½" 4"

6"

17½"

32½"

8½"

10"

6"

4"   16"   4"

② REAR ELEVATION
SCALE: 3/32" = 1"

PROVIDE 19" METAL "PINS" FOR
ANCHORING PURPOSES (BACK
POSTS ONLY)

12"

③ SIDE ELEVATION
SCALE: 3/32" = 1"

54"

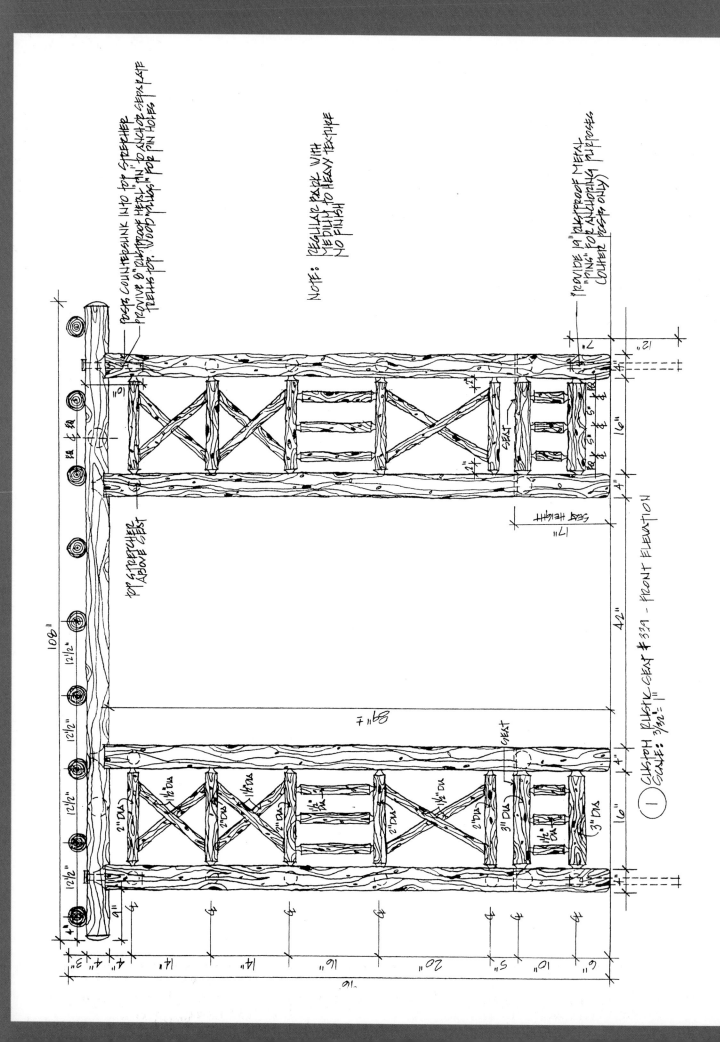

NOTE: REGULAR BARK WITH MEDIUM TO HEAVY TEXTURE
NO FINISH

POSTS COUNTERSINK INTO TOP STRETCHER
PROVIDE 8" RUSTPROOF METAL "PIN" TO SECURE POSTS INTO BOTTOM STRETCHER

TOP STRETCHER ABOVE SEAT

PROVIDE 1" RUSTPROOF METAL "PIN" FOR ATTACHING COUNTER TOP

① CUSTOM RUSTIC SEAT #379 - FRONT ELEVATION
SCALE: 3/32" = 1"

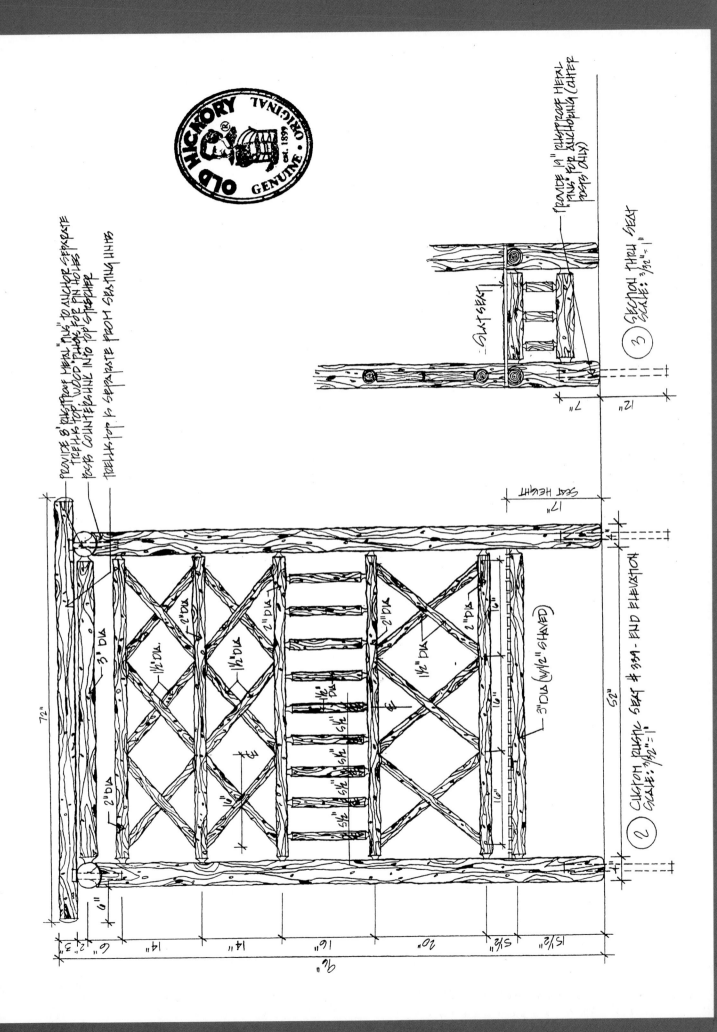

galleries and
other sources

THE RALPH KYLLOE GALLERY
P.O. BOX 669
LAKE GEORGE, NY 12845
518-696-4100

STICKS AND STONES
3680 GALLERIA
EDINA, MN 55435
612-926-5337

ADIRONDACK STORE AND GALLERY
109 SARANAC AVENUE
LAKE PLACID, NY 12946
518-523-2646